OTHER BOOKS FROM KANE/MILLER

One Woolly Wombat

The Magic Bubble Trip

The House From Morning to Night

Wilfrid Gordon McDonald Partridge

Brush

I Want My Potty

Girl From the Snow Country

Cat In Search of a Friend

The Truffle Hunter

Goodbye Rune

The Umbrella Thief

Winnie the Witch

The Park Bench

Sorry, Miss Folio!

The Night of the Stars

Paul and Sebastian

The Tram to Bondi Beach

Hanimations

The Cat Hat

For Vanessa Rachel who likes to laugh
A.B.

First American Edition 1989 by Kane/Miller Book Publishers
Brooklyn, N.Y. & La Jolla, California

Originally published in Germany under the title *Ein Wunderlicher Rat*
by Verlag Heinrich Ellermann, Munich, Germany.

Copyright © 1989 Verlag Heinrich Ellermann, Munich, Germany
American text copyright © 1989 Kane/Miller Book Publishers

Library of Congress Cataloging in Publication Data is available:

Brodmann, Aliana.
  Such a noise!

  Translation of: Ein wunderlicher Rat.
  Summary: Unable to stand his overcrowded and noisy
home any longer, a poor man goes to the Rabbi for advice.
  [1. Folklore, Jewish] I. Poppel, Hans, ill.
II. Title.
PZ8.1.B78Su   1989   398.21'089'924   89-15248
ISBN 0-916291-25-1

Printed in Germany
1   2   3   4   5   6   7   8   9   10

Such A Noise!

A *Jewish Folktale*

Retold by Aliana Brodmann
Illustrations by Hans Poppel

*Translated by Aliana Brodmann
and David Fillingham*

A C R A N K Y   N E L L   B O O K

KM Kane/Miller Book Publishers

Brooklyn, New York & La Jolla, California

A farmer once lived in a small hut at the edge of the woods with his wife, seven children and a housemaid.

Each day with the first crowing of the rooster, he would be driven out into the fields, because as soon as the children were up and about, they would begin to squabble. The housemaid would scurry about trying to keep the children apart while his wife would yell and scream at them all day long.

One morning the farmer became so fed up with all the noise, and found all the ranting and raging so unbearable, he thought he wouldn't be able to stand it another minute. So he saddled his horse and rode into the village to ask the Rabbi for his advice.

"I came here," explained the farmer to the Rabbi, "because I can't stand it at home any longer. It's so crowded that we're always bumping into each other, and the arguments never stop. The children are constantly bickering, and the maid never stops yakking."

The Rabbi listened carefully. Finally he turned to the farmer and asked him, "Do you have any chickens?"

"Of course I have chickens," replied the farmer, "three fat hens and a fine rooster."

"Then this is my advice," said the Rabbi. "Ride home as fast as you can and immediately bring the hens and the rooster into the house."

The Rabbi's advice seemed pretty strange to the farmer, but he was so desperate for some peace and quiet, that he did as he was told. He rode back to his farm and brought the hens and rooster out of the chicken coop and into the house.

After a few days it became clear that the situation in the hut was not getting any better, but had actually taken a turn for the worse. On top of the usual daily bickering and strife was now added the mad crowing of the bewildered rooster and the cackling of the brooding hens.

Confused, the farmer returned to the Rabbi and told him his advice hadn't worked very well.

"On the contrary," he explained, "the rooster crows and the hens cackle on top of everything else. It's unbearable."

The Rabbi stroked his beard thoughtfully. "So tell me," he said finally, "perhaps you have a few geese?"

"Geese?" exclaimed the farmer. "Of course I have geese! A whole gaggle of geese!"

"I thought so," said the Rabbi. "As soon as you get home, bring your geese into the house as well."

"In with the chickens?" asked the farmer.

"Exactly," responded the Rabbi. "With the chickens."

So the farmer did as he was told. As soon as he got back home, he ran across the yard and drove the geese into the house. Their wild honking mixed in with the cackling of the hens and the crowing of the rooster.

"Have you gone mad?" the farmer's wife asked him.

The housemaid grumbled, and the children were worse than ever.

The next day the farmer again went to the Rabbi to complain. "The geese aren't helping at all," he said. "My head is ringing with all the noise that I have had to endure."

The Rabbi nodded sympathetically. "You have to trust me," he said, "otherwise nothing will work out."

"But of course I trust you," answered the farmer.

"All right," replied the Rabbi, "now you surely have a cow, haven't you?"

"The best milk cow far and wide!" said the farmer.

"Fine," said the Rabbi. "Then take the cow into the house with you too."

"Wait . . . ," pleaded the farmer.

But the Rabbi had already withdrawn into his rear chamber, so the farmer had no choice but to drag his reluctant cow out of the barn and into the house.

The cow settled down before the open fire frightening the chickens and the geese. The room was filled with a deafening cackling, screeching, crowing, honking and mooing that lasted all night long.

The tormented farmer found himself before the Rabbi once again. "No, no, no," he moaned. "I'll go crazy if this monstrous noise doesn't stop soon."

"Then something must be done immediately," declared the Rabbi with enthusiasm.

"IMMEDIATELY," the farmer repeated.

"So what about goats?" inquired the Rabbi. "Do you have goats?"

The farmer gulped.

"Well?" asked the Rabbi.

"Well . . . just three," replied the farmer somewhat hesitantly.

"Then you have no choice," said the rabbi, " but to bring the three goats into your home at once."

"You can't be serious," protested the farmer.

"Would I joke about something as serious as that?" responded the Rabbi. "Now get going. Hurry so that you get home before dark."

With a sense of gloom, the farmer rode home. Obediently he brought the goats from the pasture and into the house, only to be met with the scorn and ridicule of his wife and the maid.

"I'm just following the Rabbi's advice," he explained feebly. "You can ask him if you want . . ."

The screaming, trampling, mooing, cackling and honking of the next few days was unimaginable. Ragged chicken feathers floated in the air. Shmushed eggs oozed down the walls. Cow dung was all over the place. The rooster crowed and the goats jumped about wildly.

The farmer rode back to the Rabbi at a full gallop.

"I implore you," the farmer moaned, "it is worse than ever. My head's going to explode from this madness which has become the daily routine. My wife curses me and blames me for everything. This is no way to live!"

The Rabbi listened patiently, cradling his head first in one hand and then the other.

"So say something," the farmer urged.

"Well," replied the Rabbi, "we can't avoid it. You'll have to bring your horse into the house, if only for a day."

"Oh no!" the poor farmer protested.

"You're giving up?" asked the Rabbi raising his eyebrows.

"No," answered the farmer, "of course not. But do you really think that bringing my horse into the house is going to help?"

"Why else would I have suggested it?" said the Rabbi with an encouraging wink.

That evening the farmer, with a heart as heavy as lead, dragged his poor perplexed horse into the hut.

"Good Lord," wailed his wife, "bring my husband back to his senses. He is totally out of his mind."

The maid just glowered while the children amused themselves by tickling the horse's nostrils with goose feathers. The horse's sneezing and neighing made the walls tremble.

Words could not describe the noise and commotion that went on throughout the night. There was a cackling, stomping, neighing, mooing, trampling, screeching, honking and cursing as never before. *Such a noise!*

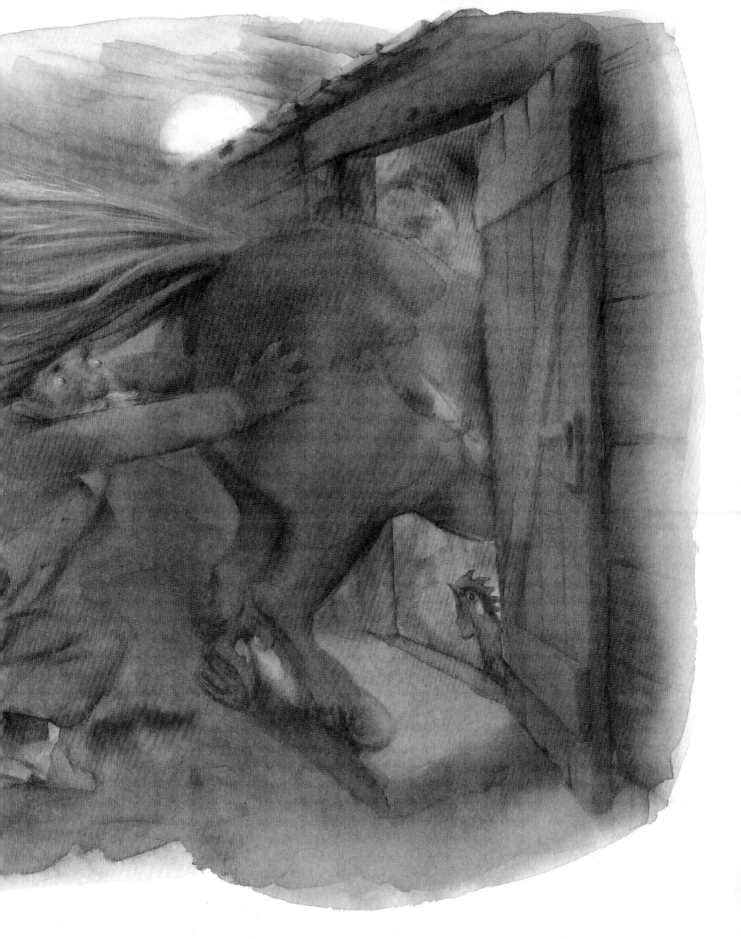

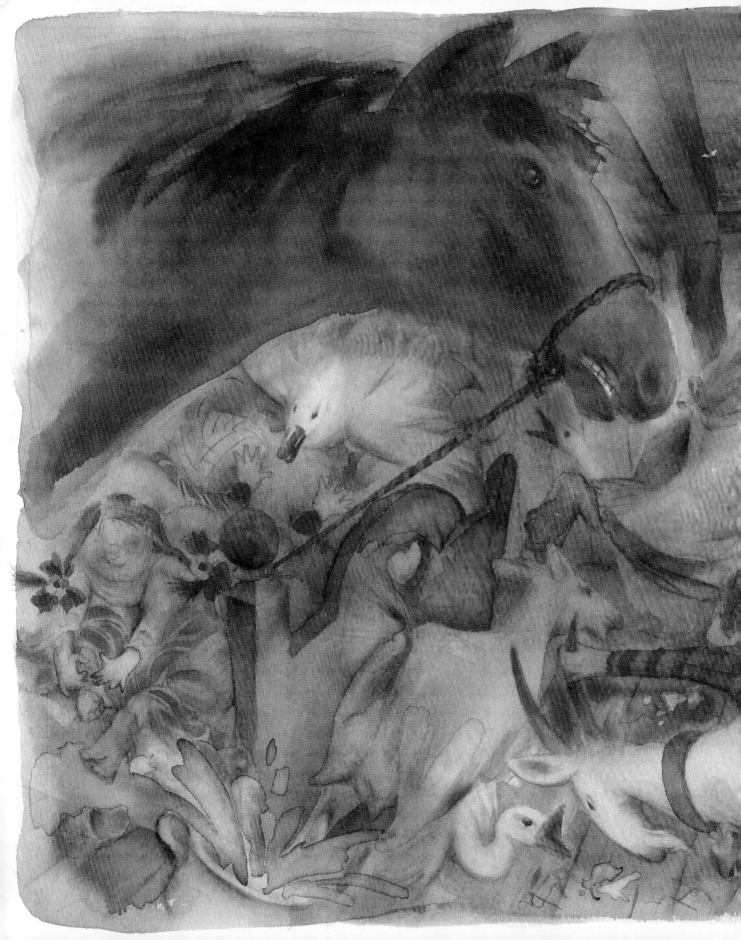

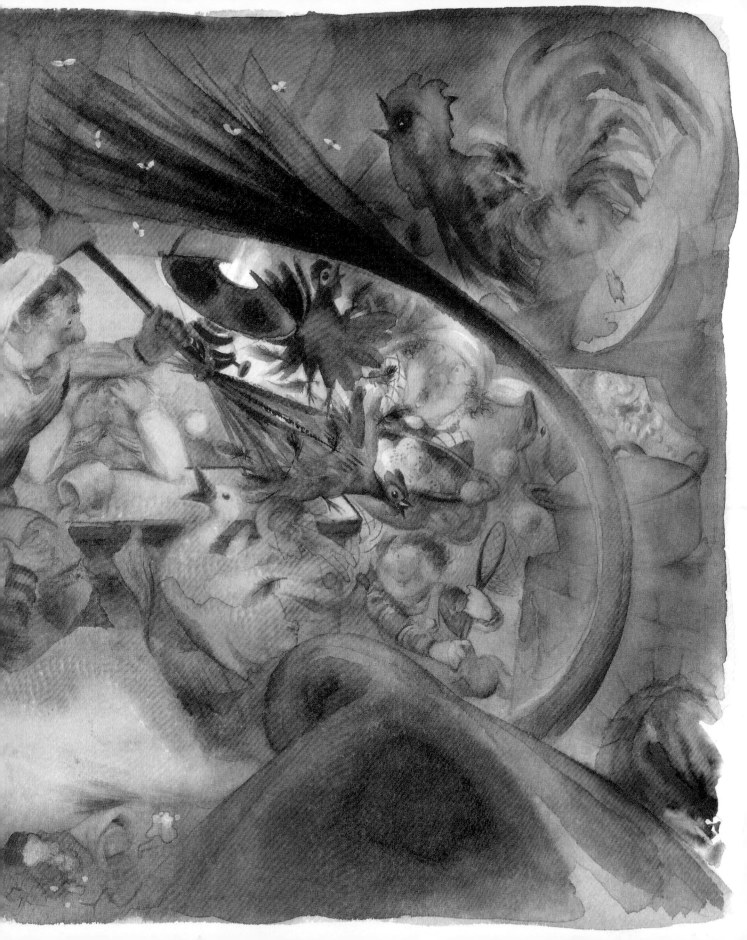

At dawn the farmer, unshaven and unkempt, ran into the village and frantically knocked on the Rabbi's door.

"Dear good wise man," begged the farmer, "open the door and rescue me. There is no room left in my house to either live or breathe!"

Finally the Rabbi opened the door. "Calm down," he said softly, "we are actually close to solving your problem."

"Really?" asked the farmer in amazement. "I already have my entire barnyard living in my hut."

"Are you sure?" demanded the Rabbi.

"Absolutely," confirmed the farmer.

"Well then," the Rabbi went on happily. "The day has finally come for you to return your horse to the field, the cow to its stable, the goats to the pasture, the geese to the yard and the hens and rooster to their coop."

Speechlessly, the farmer listened. At last, he pulled himself together and shaking his head left the house of the Rabbi.

When he arrived home, he did exactly as he had been told.
He led the horse into the field,
the cow to its stable,
the goats to the pasture,
the geese into the yard and
the chickens back into the coop.

And when he returned to the hut, there was a heavenly
silence. No neighing, no mooing, no cackling, no crowing, no
stomping, no yelling, no cursing, no fighting.

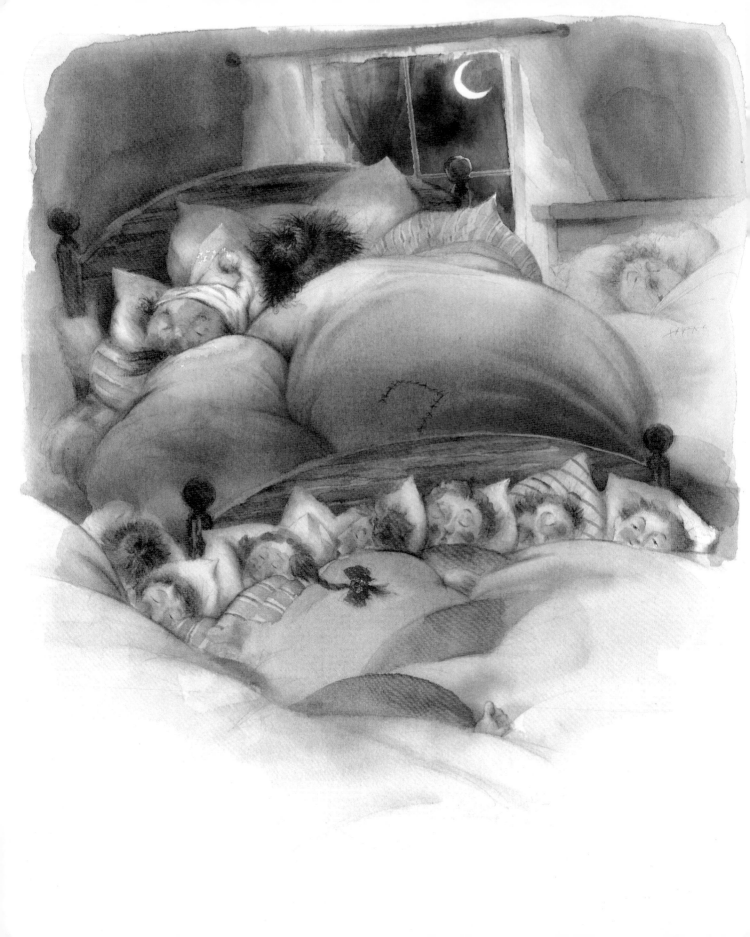

That night the family slept blissfully while the moon shone into the window.

Overjoyed, the farmer went to see the Rabbi that next morning.

"You have no idea," he explained to the Rabbi, "how peaceful life is for us now. Simply heaven on earth."